Bass 2

INTRODUCTION

Why did you buy this book, too?

You bought it because you love learning about the bass. And we're glad—it's a great instrument!

We assume that you've already completed (and reviewed a couple hundred times) *FastTrack*™ **Bass** 1. If not, please consider going through it first. (We'd hate to cover something before you're ready.)

In any case, this book picks up right where **Book 1** ended. You'll learn lots more notes, some scales and riffs, and plenty of cool techniques. And, of course, the last section of all the *FastTrack*™ books are the same so that you and your friends can form a band and jam together!

So, if you still feel ready for this book, finish your pizza, put the cat outside, take the phone off the hook, and let's jam...

Always remember the three Ps: **patience**, **practice** and **pace yourself**. We'll add one more to this list: be **proud of yourself** for a job well-done.

ABOUT THE AUDIO

We're glad you noticed the added bonus—audio tracks! Each music example in the book is included, so you can hear how it sounds and play along when you're ready. Take a listen whenever you see this symbol: ❶

Each audio example is preceded by one measure of "clicks" to indicate the tempo and meter. Pan right to hear the bass part emphasized. Pan left to hear the accompaniment emphasized. As you become more confident, try playing along with the rest of the band. (Remember to use audio track 1 [❶] to help you tune before you play.)

PLAYBACK+
Speed • Pitch • Balance • Loop

To access audio, visit:
www.halleonard.com/mylibrary

Enter Code
1854-0853-9734-4741

ISBN 978-0-7935-7546-6

HAL•LEONARD®

Visit Hal Leonard online at
www.halleonard.com

World headquarters, contact:
Hal Leonard
7777 West Bluemound Road
Milwaukee, WI 53213
Email: info@halleonard.com

In Europe, contact:
Hal Leonard Europe Limited
1 Red Place
London, W1K 6PL
Email: info@halleonardeurope.com

In Australia, contact:
Hal Leonard Australia Pty. Ltd.
4 Lentara Court
Cheltenham, Victoria, 3192 Australia
Email: info@halleonard.com.au

LESSON 1
Get in the groove!

Let's begin with something fun and easy: playing some basic grooves using many of the elements we learned in Book 1. Of course, let's not be redundant—as we review some old concepts, we'll throw in a few new ones, too. Let's get started...

Follow your roots...

As we learned in Book 1, many bass lines simply follow the root notes of the chord progression. Do just that with track 2.

REMINDER: The root note is the same as the name of the chord. C is the root of a C chord.

2 All Along the Sidewalk

Adding the fifth and octave...

In addition to the root, the **fifth** and **octave** are often used to create many standard bass lines. (Again, after Book 1, this is nothing new to you!)

3 It Used to Be Mine

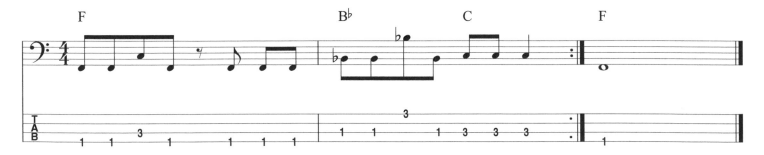

Remember the rhythmic concept of playing "off the beat?" Here's a riff using syncopation…

GOOD THING TO KNOW: The symbol "N.C." in the example below is an abbreviation for "no chord." Just as you might expect, it means that no specific chord is being played.

4 S.O.S.

Slash Chords

These are chords that indicate a specific bass note to be played. For example, C/G means to play a C chord over a G bass note. (The band plays the chord, you play the bass note!)

QUICK AND EASY: When you see a slash in a chord symbol, play the note to the right of the slash.

5 Another Hue

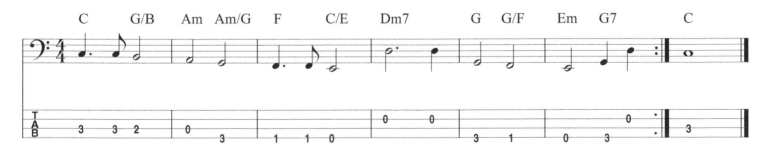

Not every note should be played the same way. So, here are a couple of variations...

Staccato

A **staccato** "dot" placed by the notehead means to play the note short. In other words, release pressure on the fretted note immediately after playing it, so it won't "ring out." Listen to track 6 to hear how it sounds.

6 Bridge

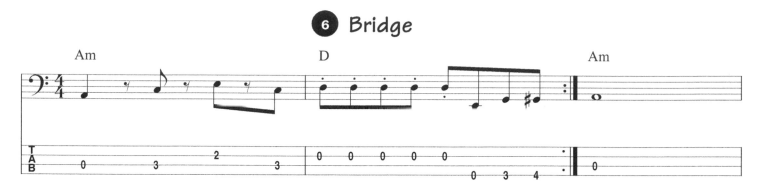

PLAYING TIP: Don't lift your finger off the string!
Just stop sounding the note by releasing the pressure on the string.

Palm Muting

The symbol "P.M." under the notes (between the staff and TAB) is short-hand for **palm muting**. This is done by using the heel of your picking hand to muffle (or "mute") the strings. When done correctly, you'll notice a thicker, more percussive sound.

NOTE: Palm muting works best for pick-style bassists.

7 Muted Groove

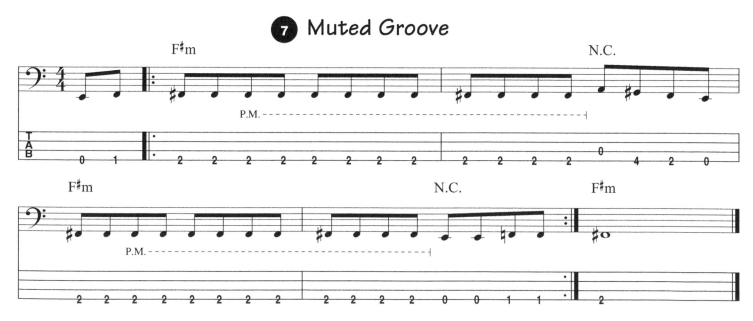

We'll learn more playing variations as we go through the book, but DON'T SKIP AHEAD!

LESSON 2

Back to the basics...

Very briefly, let's take some time to review the note positions we learned in Book 1 (and add some finishing touches)...

First Position Review

The area of the neck from the open strings to fret 4 is called **first position**. The diagram and note chart below cover all of the notes in this area.

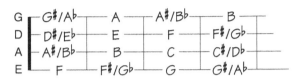

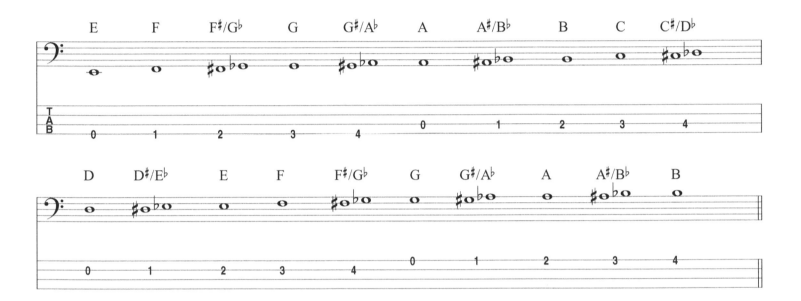

 IMPORTANT: Some notes can have different names but occupy the same fret (for example, F# and Gb). These are referred to as **enharmonic equivalents**. Either spelling (note name) is acceptable.

Let's try some bass lines using the notes in first position...

8 Blues-Rock

5

Here are a few more in first position...

9 Anthem Rock

NOTE: The next song has a **1st** and **2nd ending** (indicated by brackets and the numbers "1" and "2"). Play the song once to the repeat sign (1st ending), then repeat from measure 2. The second time through, skip the 1st ending and play the 2nd (last) ending.

10 Hey, Jim

Don't worry about chord symbols you don't recognize—we'll explain a few of them later. Your main concern right now is the notes.

11 All That Jazz

A BIT FASTER NOW

What if you want to play faster than eighth notes but in the same tempo? Welcome to the world of sixteenths.

Sixteenth Notes

These have two flags or beams: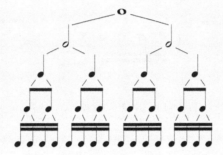

Sixteenth rests look like eighth rests but with (you're way ahead of us!) two flags: ♦

Yuck, more math...

Two sixteenths equal one eighth (just like fractions), and four sixteenths equal one quarter. Here's a diagram showing the relationship of all the rhythmic values you've learned:

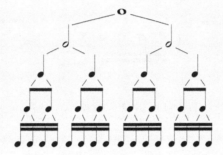

To count sixteenths, divide the beat into four by counting "1 e & a, 2 e & a, 3 e & a, 4 e & a":

1 e & a 2 e & a 3 e & a 4 e & a

Listen to Track 12 (with steady quarter note clicks throughout) to hear this new faster rhythm.

12 Progressively Faster

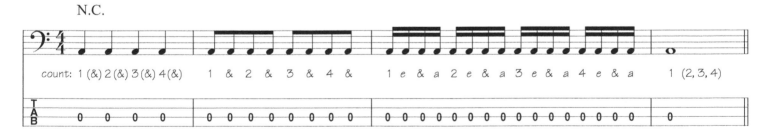

Now try playing it. Remember to play slowly at first and speed up the tempo only as it becomes easier.

That's a little hard on the right hand, huh? EASY SOLUTION: alternate downstrokes (⊓) and upstrokes (V), or alternate using your first and second fingers.

13 Nice Pants

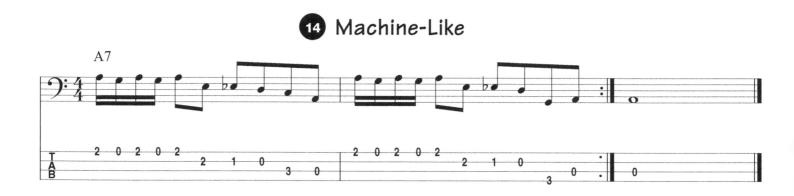

14 Machine-Like

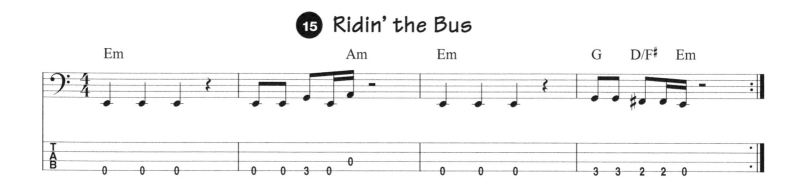

You'll often encounter two sixteenths beamed to an eighth note, like in track 15:

15 Ridin' the Bus

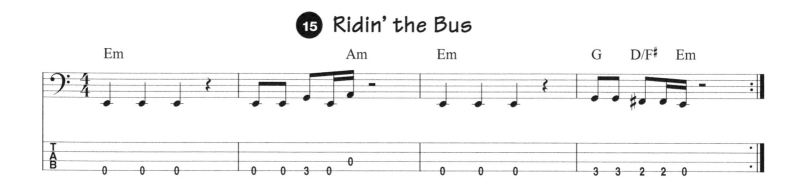

☞ We like to encourage breaks on a regular basis, and this is no exception.
Take five and we'll see you back here for Lesson 3.

LESSON 3
Keys, please...

A song's **key** is determined by the scale used to create the song. For example, a song based on the C major scale is said to be in the **key of C**. We already learned about scales in Book 1, so let's take a closer look at how scales relate to keys...

Sharps and flats are unavoidable...

Depending on the root note used, most scales contain sharps or flats. (There are two exceptions: **C major** and **A minor** have no sharps or flats.) Since keys and scales are related, a key will have the same number of sharps or flats as its corresponding scale.

Sign in, please...

A **key signature** is used at the beginning of each line of music to tell you two important things:

 Notes to play sharp or flat throughout the piece

 Song's key

For example, the key of G contains F♯, so its key signature will have one sharp on the F-line. This tells you to play all Fs as F♯ (unless, of course, you see a natural sign ♮).

Here are some common (and easy) keys...

Key of C

This one's based on the C major scale, which has no sharps or flats:

16 Slow Tune

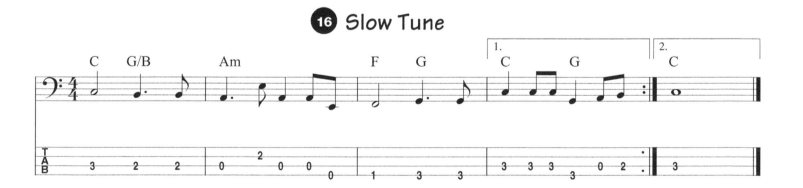

NOTE: The key of C looks like there is no key signature, since there are no sharps or flats.

Key of G

...based on the G major scale, which has one sharp—F#:

17 Jam in G

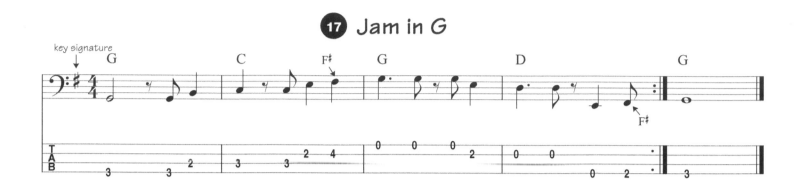

Key of F

...based on the F major scale, which has one flat—B♭:

18 Jamaican Groove

What the heck—here's one more...

Key of D

This one has two sharps (F# and C#) and is based on (you guessed it!) the D major scale:

19 Pop-Rock

LESSON 4
You've got the blues...

If you haven't heard of the **blues,** then where have you been? It's been around for ages and has been used by such music legends as B.B. King, Eric Clapton, and Muddy Waters. Blues is fun (and easy) to play.

12-Bar Form

The most typical blues uses a form called **12-bar form**. This doesn't mean that the song is only twelve bars (measures) long. Rather, the song uses several 12-bar phrases (or sections) repeated over and over.

Generally, blues songs use only three chords: the **first, fourth** and **fifth** chords of the key (indicated with Roman numerals I, IV and V). Thus, as a bass player, it's important to know the first, fourth and fifth notes of each key's scale. To find these three notes, count up the scale from the root of the key:

Key	Chord / Scale Tone							
	I			IV	V			
Blues in "C"	C	D	E	F	G	A	B	C
Blues in "F"	F	G	A	B♭	C	D	E	F
Blues in "G"	G	A	B	C	D	E	F♯	G
Blues in "D"	D	E	F♯	G	A	B	C♯	D

Listen to the following example of 12-bar blues in "G" on Track 20. Then follow the chord symbols and play along with your own bass line...

20 Blues in G

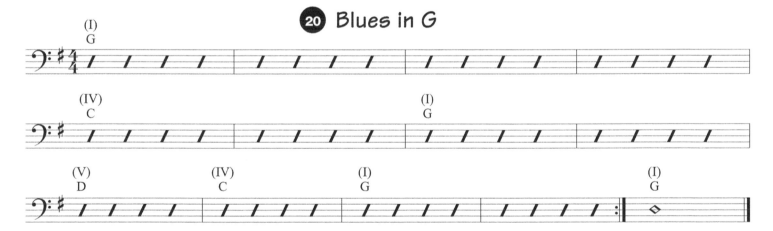

IMPORTANT: Notice the number of measures each chord is played during the 12-bar form. This is the most common 12-bar blues chord progression...

Chord		Measures
I	=	four
IV	=	two
I	=	two
V	=	one
IV	=	one
I	=	two

Turnaround, sit up, and play...

The last two bars of the 12-bar blues progression are sometimes called the **turnaround**, since they "turn" the form back "around" to the beginning. Musicians often vary the turnaround, using different chords or even a written out riff. (This is a good spot for you to throw in some fifths or octaves.)

The most common turnaround variation uses the V chord in the last measure like in the example below:

21 Riff Blues

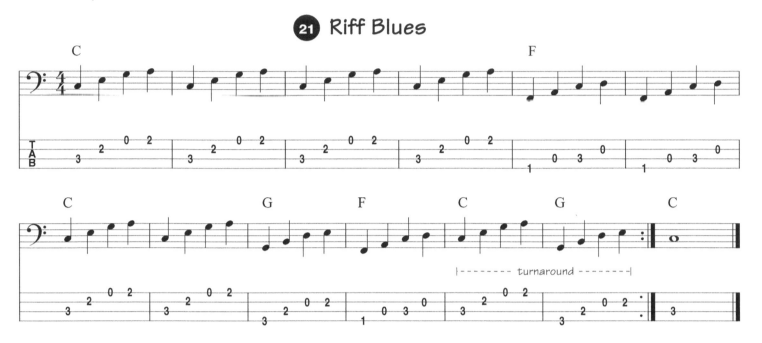

Another variation uses the IV chord in measure 2. This is called the **quick change**, since the chord progression "changes" to the IV chord and "quickly" returns to the I chord.

22 Quick Change Artist

SHUT UP AND SHUFFLE!

The **shuffle feel** is a very common element of rock, blues, pop and jazz music. It uses a new rhythmic value called a **triplet.**

Triplets

By now you know that two eighth notes equal one quarter, and four eighth notes equal one half. Guess what? Three eighth notes played in the duration of one beat (or one quarter note) is an **eighth-note triplet.**

A triplet is beamed together with a number 3:

To count a triplet, simply say the word "tri-pl-et" during one beat. Tap your foot to the beat and count out loud as you listen to track 23:

23 Tri-pl-et

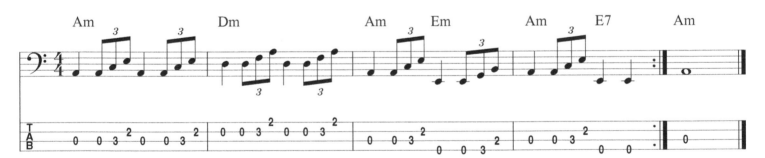

Keep tapping your foot as you listen to and follow the next bass line:

24 Minor Bird Blues

Now play it yourself. Keep thinking "tri-pl-et, tri-pl-et, tri-pl-et, tri-pl-et" as you tap your foot to the beat...

 You can also use the word "cho-co-late" to help you count triplets. (Of course, this could make you really hungry after counting a long song?!)

Triplets can also include rests. Most common is to have a rest within the triplet (between two eighth notes):

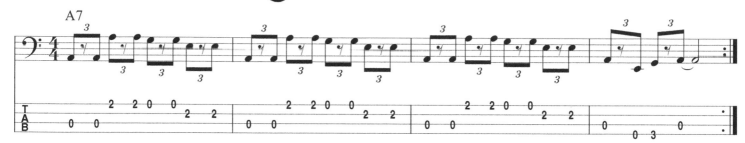

Once you get the hang of this "bouncy" feel, you'll never forget it...

26 Shuffle Groove

They say everything's bigger in Texas, so for the next one...TURN IT UP!

27 Texas Blues

3/4, 4/4, 12/8?

Until this page, you've been playing with time signatures in which the quarter note equals one beat. Let's learn something new (change is good!):

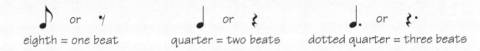

12 beats per measure
eighth note (1/8) = one beat

All notes and rests are relative to the value of an eighth note in 6/8 meter:

eighth = one beat   quarter = two beats   dotted quarter = three beats

In 12/8 meter, an eighth note equals one beat and there are twelve beats per measure. But the rhythmic **pulse** feels like there are only four beats per measure. Listen and count along to track 28, and you'll see what we mean:

28

count: 1   2   3,   4   5   6   (7 8)   9,   10   11   12

Now try a few bass lines in your new meter...

29 ## Delta Blues

30 ## Shuffling in Chicago

LISTEN AND COMPARE: The rhythmic feel of track 30 and track 27 (on the previous page) sound similar. That's because 12/8 meter is divided into groups of three eighth notes, just like triplets in 4/4 meter.

LESSON 5
A little bit higher...

In Lesson 2 we reviewed all the notes in first position. Of course, not every song can be played down there, so let's learn some higher notes...

Fifth Position

To play notes above fret 4 requires sliding up to **fifth position**, aptly named because you move up to the **fifth** fret.

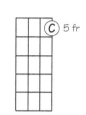

Slide your hand up the neck and place finger 1 on fret 5 to play high C.

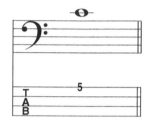

NOTE: To help you quickly find this position, you'll notice a little white dot at fret 5 on your bass neck. It's easier than counting, right?

Take a few minutes now to review the diagram below. Make sure you spend time learning where the notes are on both the fretboard and the staff. (Tell your fingers what you're playing—say each note out loud as you press it.)

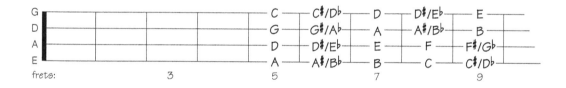

31 Fifth Position Chromatics

Not so fast—review it again!

16

To get a better grip on this new position, try a few scales...

32 C Major Scale

33 A Minor Scale

Scales are good exercises, but riffs sound great up here, too...

34 Water Chestnut

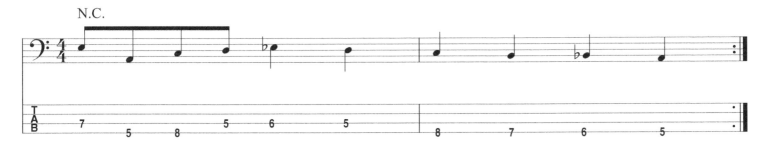

The next one uses an open string (low E) while your left hand stays in fifth position for the rest of the riff:

35 Zodiak

Keep it slow and fun, so you don't get frustrated!

When to change...

Generally speaking, if you're going to play up high for a while, stay in fifth position. Too much unnecessary sliding will tire you out (and sound clumsy).

If you don't have TAB to show you the convenient positions to play a song, it's a good idea to survey each song before you play and mark appropriate spots to change positions. Players often use Roman numerals (I and V) to mark these spots—in fact, so do we...

36 King of Spades

Squeaky clean...

You may notice your hand making a little "squeaking" sound as you move between positions. Don't worry about it. In fact, you'll notice this sound is pretty common in almost all pop and rock recordings. But don't cause a blister—release left-hand pressure as you move between positions.

Take a break—call a friend and have them learn another **FastTrack**™ instrument. But don't dial too fast...you're supposed to rest those fingers!

LESSON 6

The shape of things to come...

In order to create your own bass lines, you need to learn more about chords—which notes relate to which chords...and why!

First things first...

Generally, guitarists and keyboard players play the chords of a song. Bassists don't (normally) play chords—rather, they play "broken" chords, or the notes of a chord one note at a time. (This is called an **arpeggio**, if you prefer Italian.)

Each arpeggio you play has a **movable shape**. That is, you can use the same hand position and play up and down the neck of your bass to accommodate any chord or key. The fingerboard chart below gives you all the notes on the first twelve frets of strings 3 and 4:

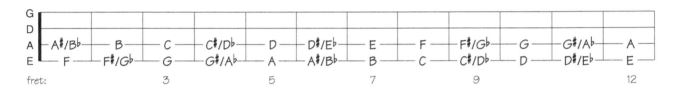

Let's learn some shapes and prove this "movable" theory...

Octave Shapes

The most important shape to know is the octave (which you know is eight notes apart from the root). Every note has an octave above or below (or both).

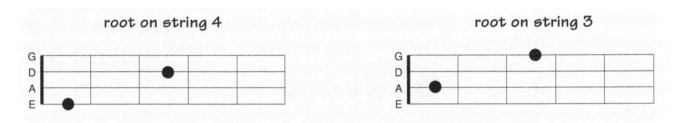

root on string 4   root on string 3

Now, apply the **movable shape theory**. Locate C on either string 4 or 3 and apply the correct shape from above. Play each fretted note (a C octave). Now slide up two frets to D and play both notes (a D octave). Now apply this to a bass line:

37 Easy Octave

Major Chord Shapes

Major chords contain the **root, third** and **fifth** notes of the major scale:

On the fretboard, these notes translate to our next movable arpeggio shape...

Let's try a few common bass lines using the major chord arpeggio shape.

38 Standard '50s

Now add the octave shape...

39 Medium Rock

Try more arpeggios on other major chords. Simply find the shape and slide your hand up and down to the desired root—F, F♯, B♭, D, etc.

Minor Chord Shapes

Minor chords contain the **root**, a **flatted third**, and **fifth** notes of the major scale:

Major scale: C—D—E—F—G—A—B—C

Minor chord arpeggio: C—E♭—G

...which translates to the following shape on the fretboard:

40 Sad Song

This next one uses the fifth of Dm (the note A) in both of its octave positions...

41 Latin Groove

A few more...

Here are some more movable patterns. They aren't really specific to any particular type of chord—they just sound cool! Notice the shape of each and keep these handy in your "bag of tricks" when making up your own bass line accompaniments...

42 Easy Groovin'

43 Wrap It Up

44 Rock 'n' Roll

45 Move Over

 Time for another break! You owe it to yourself (and to your poor fingers).
Knitting would not be a good activity during this break?!

LESSON 7

Locking in with the drummer...

An important part of being a good bass player is listening to (and sometimes playing along with) the drummer. The two of you are the basic instruments of the **rhythm section**, and it's your jobs to lay a tight and solid rhythmic foundation for the rest of the band.

With the Bass Drum

Focusing on the bass drum is a great place to start. Track 46 demonstrates a common ballad feel. Notice how the bass and bass drum emphasize a similar rhythmic pattern:

46 Follow the Bass Drum

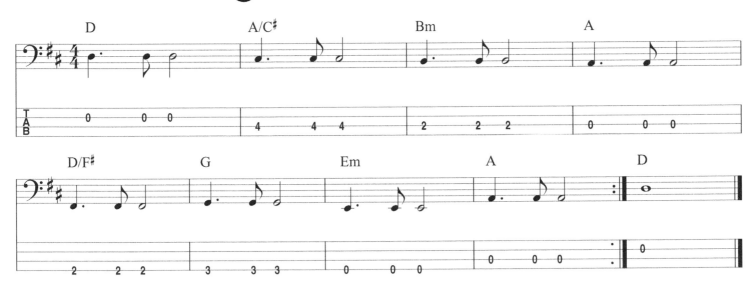

Now try the same thing but with an up-tempo rock feel...

47 Kick It!

Play it again and substitute some octaves.

Many bass lines alternate to the fifth of the chord as the drummer strikes the snare drum.
Listen to this in track 48 before playing it yourself...

48 Yer Basic Ballad

Notice the movable shape of the next bass line—another one for your "bag of tricks!"

49 Bass Ostinato

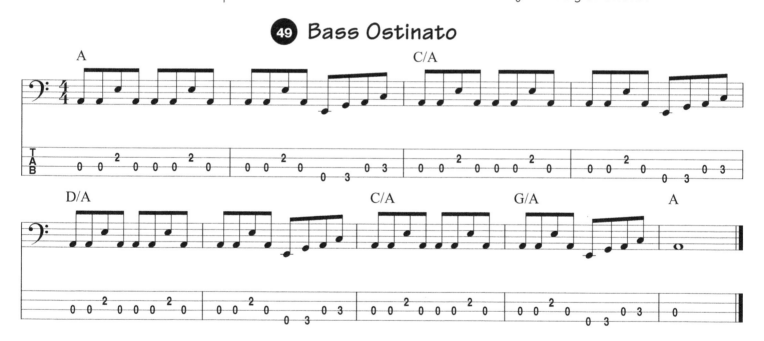

That ain't all...

Explore other ways to play with the drummer. For example:

  Play an octave leap every time the drummer hits a crash cymbal.

  Play eighth notes along with the hi-hat or ride cymbal.

  Stop playing! That's right, play nothing as the drummer strikes the snare.

Anticipation

Anticipation is another type of syncopation. It occurs when the band (all together, not separately) plays a new chord change just before a downbeat. In other words, the chord "hit" is displaced by the preceding offbeat—the chord is anticipated.

Track 50 is a good example of this. Pay special attention to beat 4 of measures 1 and 3. Sounds like beat 1 of the next measure is being played early...

50 Catch the Kicks

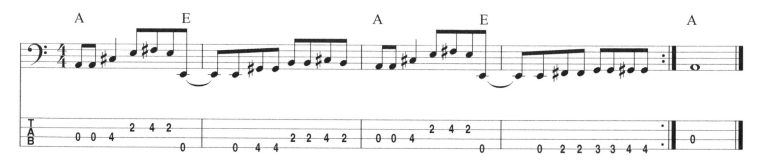

51 Still Can't Wait

Speaking of anticipation—you can't wait to go buy **FastTrack**™ **Bass Songbook 2**. It's loaded with hits like "Back in the U.S.S.R.," "Born to be Wild," and "Layla."

LESSON 8

Let's get fancy...

You've been so patient, learning your notes, scales, and patterns. Now's a great time to experiment and learn some "tricks of the trade"—some **slur techniques** that you've probably heard but didn't know how to do.

Slur techniques (or "legato" techniques, as they say in Italian) allow you to play more than one note for each pick attack. In other words, you'll be able to pick the string once and "slur" two or more notes, giving you a smooth, flowing sound. Here are a few of the most common ones...

Slide

...looks like this:

Just like it sounds—play the first note by picking the string, then sound the second note by sliding the same finger up or down on the same string. (The second note is not attacked!)

Now try using slides in some riffs...

52 Slidin' and Glidin'

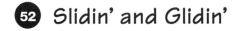

53 My Groove

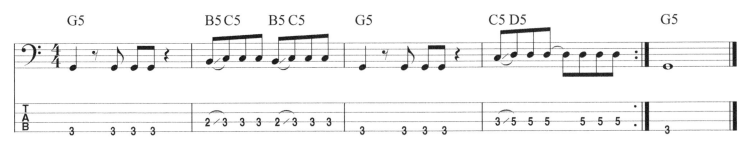

This will take some time to get the hang of, so don't be too hard on yourself.

Now try a longer slide...

54 **Wild Slide**

Slides are sometimes notated with just a short line before or after the note. This also tells you the direction to slide (up or down) to or from a note, but the length of the slide is not exact. Usually, it means to slide one or two frets.

55 **Slide This!**

Pickup and slide...

A really nice effect is to use a slide as a pickup at the start of a song. For example, start a fifth above your first note of the song and slide into the note one beat before the song (as if there was a one-beat pickup measure). Count "1, 2, 3, slide" and play the song. Track 56 is a good example:

56 **Pick You Up**

...looks like this:

Again, just like it sounds! The first note is picked, then use another finger as a "hammer" to press down onto the fret of the second (higher) note on the same string.

NOTE: You can only hammer "up" from a lower note to a higher note.

PLAYING TIP: If you hammer too hard, your fingertips will hurt; too soft and you won't hear anything. Practice and practice some more until you think you've got it.

57 Hammer Jam

58 Frightful

28

Pull-off

...looks like this:

This one is the direct opposite of the hammer-on. Start with both fingers on their notes, pick the string and then tug or "pull" your higher note finger off the string to sound the lower note.

Listen and try it in a short riff...

59 Push and Pull

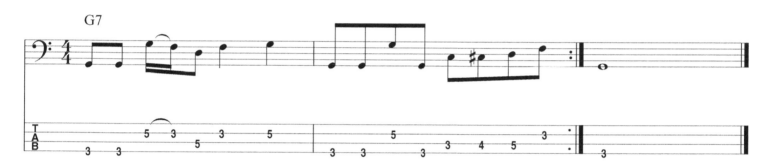

60 Steady-Pullin' Groove

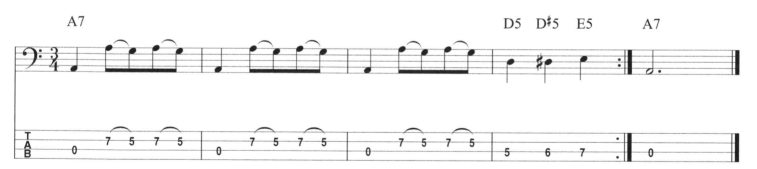

NOTE: In theory, it may be the direct opposite of the hammer-on, but it's a completely different technique. Be patient and make sure you thoroughly practice this one.

LESSON 9

Slappin' and poppin'

Slap and pop techniques are great for adding a "percussive punch" to your playing (talk about playing along with the drummer?!). Funk, pop, soul, rock, and fusion music all use the **slap** and **pop** to spice up the sound and groove. You can, too...

Slap

...looks like this:

Attack or "slap" the string with the side of your thumb (at the joint), using motion from your wrist, not your arm. Let your thumb rebound immediately (and rotate your wrist away) to allow the note to "ring" out.

☞ PLAYING TIP: As shown in the photo above, slap the string at the end of the fingerboard.

For starters, practice slapping quarter notes on the open strings:

61 All Thumbs

62 Slap This!

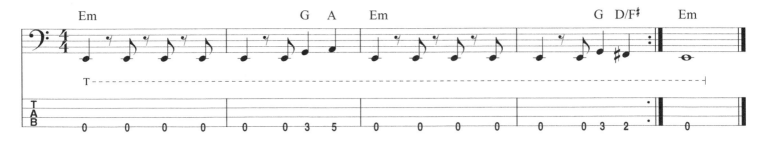

Don't get frustrated. Getting a good slap sound takes lots of practice.

63 Funky

The next one combines thumb slaps and regular fingered notes.

64 Thumbs Down

Pop

...looks like this:

Pull or "snap" the string away from the fingerboard with your index or middle finger. This is another harsh, percussive sound. When released, the string will naturally rebound off the body of the bass and "ring" out.

☞ PLAYING TIP: Keep your right-hand fingers curled and in position to pop. Also, pivot your wrist, not your arm, as you pull the string.

65 Snap, Crackle, Pop

Here are three examples combining the slap and pop (don't hurt yourself!)...

66 Poppin' Octaves

67 Slap Bass

68 Slap-Pop Groove

Handle with care...

If you haven't already figured them out, here are three precautions:

1 Don't slap too hard—bass strings are tougher than the skin on your thumb!

2 Don't pop too hard—you'll be heading to the store to buy a new string!

3 Don't slap your bandmates!

After all that slapping and popping, you may be feeling a bit "edgy"...
it's definitely time for another break!

LESSON 10
You gotta have style!

How you play is as important (if not more important) than what you play. In this lesson, we'll show you some common styles used in today's music. You can apply these styles to almost any song.

As we introduce each style, notice how following musical elements change:

 Chord progression

 Rhythmic groove

 Note choice

Rock 'n' Roll

Rock music comes in many styles—classic rock, blues rock, easy rock, hard rock, heavy metal. Its roots date from the 1950s with such legends as Elvis Presley, Jerry Lee Lewis, and The Beatles. Track 69 is an example of '50s rock 'n' roll. Listen and then play along:

69 *Golden Oldies*

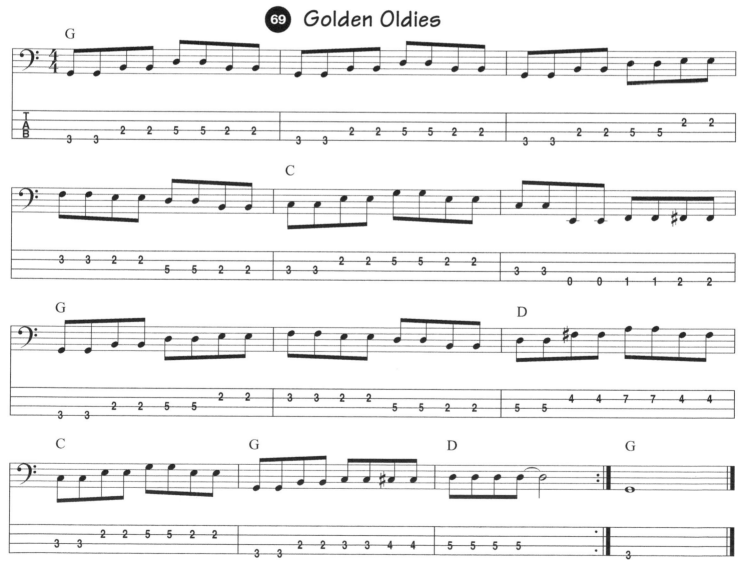

Moving up through the decades, rock music transformed into a harder sound found in the music of Led Zeppelin, Van Halen, and Metallica. The following examples imitate a hard rock and heavy metal style:

70 Rock Solid

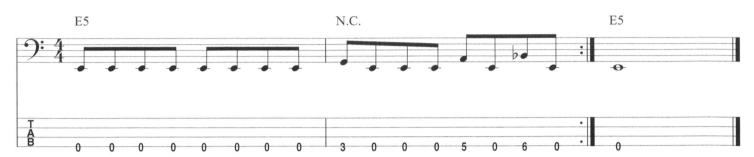

71 Dark Metal

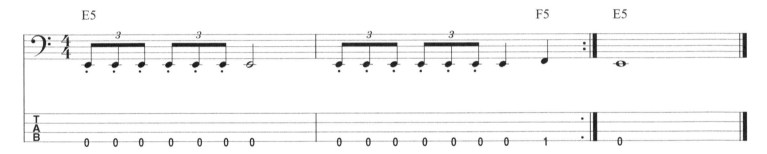

72 Glam Rock

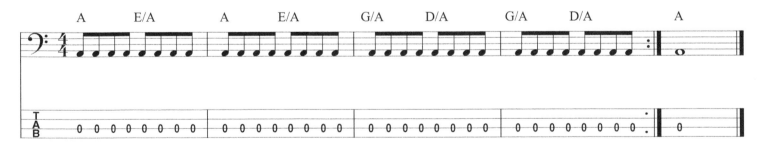

Pop (short for "popular") covers a wide spectrum of music. Sometimes called "adult contemporary," this style is used by artists like Whitney Houston, Sting, and Mariah Carey. This style is typically very melodic and employs common chord progressions like the following examples:

73 Top 40 Ballad

74 Pop-Rock Bass

Alternative Rock

In the '90s, a new style of rock music was made very popular by such bands as Nirvana, Pearl Jam, and Soundgarden. Alternative (or "Grunge") rock really has no rules as to chord progression or rhythm—anything goes! However, the following examples are common alternative sounds:

75 Chain-link

76 Just a Slice

R&B is the short way of saying "rhythm & blues." It's also sometimes called "soul." You'll find this style in the music of Stevie Wonder, Marvin Gaye, The Temptations, and many others.

77 Motown Groove

78 R&B Bass

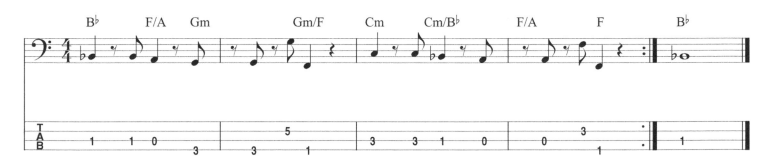

Reggae was born on the small island of Jamaica. This unique music style, played by such legends as Bob Marley and Jimmy Cliff, has been influential on music throughout the world.

Notice the common rhythm used in reggae style—emphasizing beats 2 and 4:

79 Hot in the Sun

80 Jamaican Me Crazy

Funk style can be found in anything from R&B to pop to alternative. You've heard of James Brown, Prince, Rick James, and The Red Hot Chili Peppers, right? They've all used funk style. Listen to all three of these tracks several times until you get that "funky feeling"...

NOTE: **Dotted eighth notes** are often beamed to a sixteenth. Remember, the dot adds one-half of the value, so a dotted eighth equals the length of three sixteenths. This rhythm is very common in funk style.

81 Get Funky

82 Staccato Funk

The next one's got some big leaps and hammer-ons—take it slow at first!

83 Slap Happy

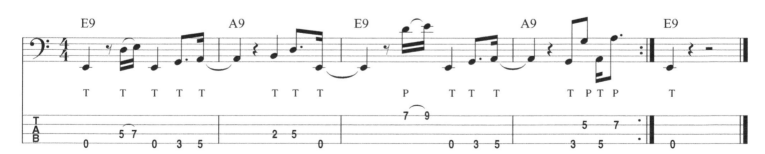

An American original—jazz features improvisation, complex chord harmony, and a variety of rhythms. Musicians like Duke Ellington, Charlie Parker, and Miles Davis have all been influential on jazz. Many variants have grown from this style, including swing, Dixieland, bebop, Latin-jazz, and fusion.

Generally speaking, anything goes in jazz music. However, there are some common elements—for example, the **walking bass line** in track 84:

84 Walk on Over

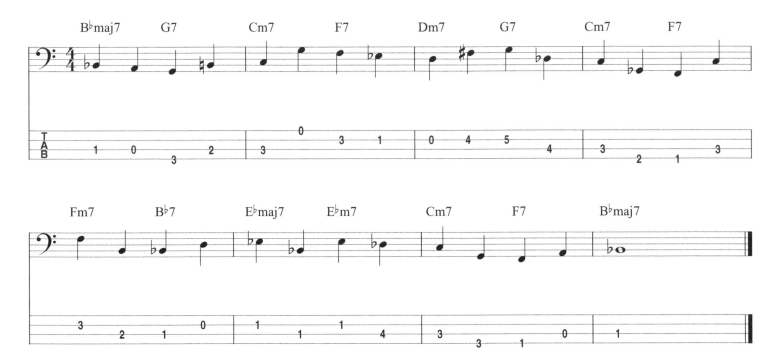

The bossa nova uses lots of fifths and octaves:

85 Who's the Bossa Nova?

Let's not forget our friends in Nashville—country music dates back from even before rock 'n' roll. Its form is usually simpler and more "laid back," although many of today's country artists like Garth Brooks, Reba McEntire, and Shania Twain incorporate some rock styles in their music.

Note the heavy use of root-fifth bass movement in the next two examples...

86 Country Boy

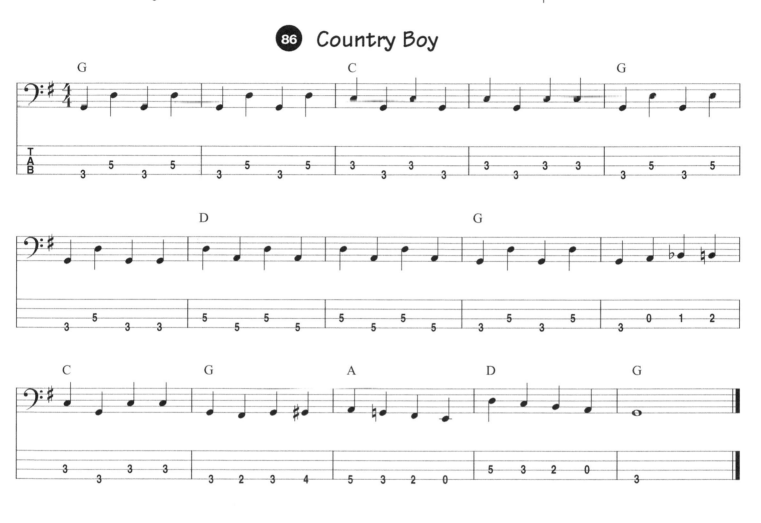

87 Tennessee Rock

Disco

Say what you want, but disco just won't die! It came and went in the '70s but resurfaced in the '90s as a major influence on today's dance music. This undeniably unique style incorporates fast rhythms and bass lines similar to this next example:

88 Disco Daze

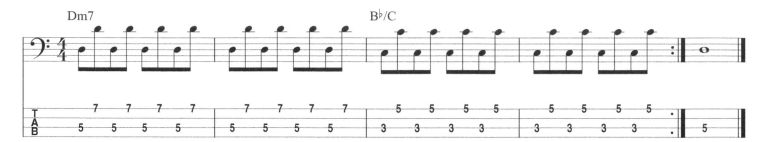

Hip-Hop

A descendant of rap music, the hip-hop style is heavily influenced by reggae, R&B, funk, and (sometimes) rock. Such artists as Snoop Doggy Dogg, TLC, Warren G, and many others have made hip-hop a mainstream musical style.

You should love it—it's (almost) always heavy on the bass line…

89 Don't Stop Hip-Hop

90 Lay Off!

LESSON 11

Strike up the band...

As in the first book, this last section isn't a lesson...it's your jam session!

All the **FastTrack**™ books (Guitar, Keyboard, Bass and Drums) have the same last section. This way, you can either play by yourself along with the audio or form a band with your friends.

So, whether the band's on the audio track or in your garage, let the show begin...

Basement Jam

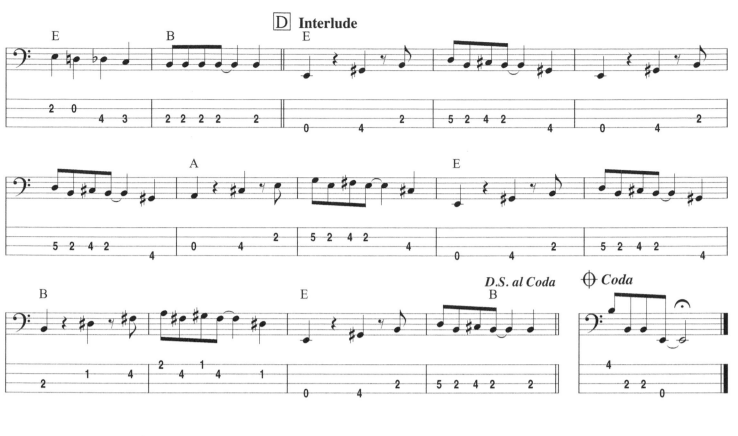

Dim the Lights

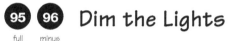

full band / minus bass

Congratulations!
You're ready for the big leagues...

A FAREWELL GIFT

(...it's the least we could do!)

We expect you to use the entire book as a reference, but this has now become a tradition—a "cheat sheet" with all the notes and arpeggio shapes you learned. Don't forget to practice often!

Notes in Fifth Position:

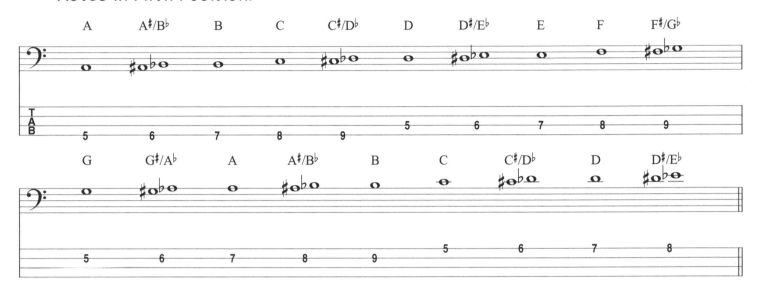

Movable Arpeggio Shapes:

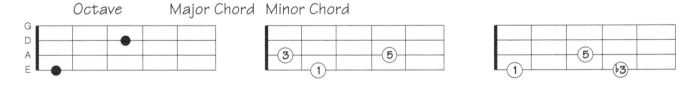

What's next?

You've started to master the bass in just a short time, but where do you go now?

 Practice, practice, practice. What more can we say but practice every day?

 Listen to everything. Turn on your radio, TV, CD player, stereo, anything musical. Learn the bass lines you like, whether it's by ear or with the sheet music.

 Buy **FastTrack™ Bass Songbooks 1 & 2**, featuring songs in rock score format by such artists as Eric Clapton, Elton John, The Beatles, and many more.

 Enjoy what you do. If you don't enjoy what you're doing, there's no sense in doing it.

Bye for now...

SONG INDEX
(...gotta have one!)